Angels All Around Us

by Sandy Colledge

Copyright © 2005 by Sandy Colledge

Angels All Around Us
by Sandy Colledge

Printed in the United States of America

ISBN 1-597810-18-5

All rights reserved solely by the author. The author guarantees all contents are original and do not infringe upon the legal rights of any other person or work. No part of this book may be reproduced in any form without the permission of the author. The views expressed in this book are not necessarily those of the publisher.

Scripture quotations taken from the Amplified® Bible, Copyright © 1954, 1958, 1962, 1964, 1965, 1987 by The Lockman Foundation. Used by permission. (www.Lockman.org)

www.xulonpress.com

Acknowledgments

To the precious Holy Spirit, our Helper, Teacher, Spirit of Truth, I give Thee thanks!

Also, many thanks to Karen Pannella for giving me a quiet place to write my books, and to Robert Schepsis, who has supported me for many years on the street when I didn't know where my next quarter (for the meters) was to come from. Many thanks also to those who "hosted" me in many cities along the way. Our combined reward is going to be great in Heaven!

And I saw a strong angel announcing in a loud voice, Who is worthy to open the scroll? And [who is entitled and deserves and is morally fit] to break its seals?
(Revelation 5:2)

Preface

Isn't it wonderful to know that we have "heavenly help" at all times? Sometimes we can see into the Spirit; sometimes we must take it by faith that angels are there to help us and to deliver a message from the throne of God. Nevertheless, they are mentioned many times in Scripture, and we will occasionally have the pleasure and reassurance that we are being kept by God's messengers.

Enjoy some more revelation along that line.

                          Sandy Colledge
                          Summer 2004

Angels unaware. How wonderful to know that
God has sent heavenly messengers to watch
over all our ways.

Are not the angels all ministering spirits (servants) sent out in the service [of God for the assistance] of those who are to inherit salvation?
(Hebrews 1:14)

When He [the Lamb] broke open the seventh seal, there was silence for about half an hour in heaven. Then I saw the seven angels who stand before God, and to them were given seven trumpets. And another angel came and stood over the altar. He had a golden censer, and he was given very much incense (fragrant spices and gums which exhale perfume when burned), that he might mingle it with the prayers of all the people of God (the saints) upon the golden altar before the throne. And the smoke of the incense (the perfume) arose in the presence of God, with the prayers of the people of God (the saints), from the hand of the angel.
(Revelation 8:1–4)

In January 1980, I was stuck—I was a brand-new Christian determined to trust God in every circumstance. Little did I know that I was going to need an angel that day.

You see, it had snowed heavily the night before, and my son and I were coming out of church on a beautiful cold morning, only to be greeted with a stubborn problem that needed divine intervention. In the interim of the church service, the snow had melted around my car and we were stuck, unable—even with the kind assistance of the other parishioners—to get the car rocked out of its ice bed! I said out loud, "What I need right now is an angel to help us get out of this mess!" I then turned around, and there, with a most beautiful smile and shoulder-length brown wavy hair and a royal blue jogging suit, with a crimson stripe running down both sides, was a *being* with a glorious face. Never speaking a word, he simply placed one index finger on the trunk of the car, causing the car to leap out of the snow bank! I turned to tell my little boy to get back into the car, and then I turned back to thank my "helper," only to discover him gone—*disappeared!* There was no other car nearby, and no time in which to get around the bend in the road ahead—he had vanished! How important are *our words* and the care our heavenly Father has for us!

Beware that you do not despise or feel scornful toward or think little of one of these little ones, for I tell you that in heaven their angels always are in the presence of and look upon the face of My Father Who is in heaven.
(Matthew 18:10)

It is such a blessing that angels are sent to help us, and each of us has at least four of them, all with names. I don't know the names of my angels, but I do know that I love to see them.

Once, driving along to a camp meeting with several children in tow, I happened to glance in the back of the car, only to see a huge angel. He was so big he took up the whole back seat. His head had the face of an eagle, and he had feathers on each side of his face. He looked at me and smiled. Of course I was startled to see how big he was, but I was reassured that he was there for our protection!

But the men [the angels] reached out and pulled Lot into the house to them and shut the door after him. And they struck the men who were at the door of the house with blindness [which dazzled them], from the youths to the old men, so that they wearied themselves [groping] to find the door. And the [two] men asked Lot, Have you any others here—sons-in-law or your sons or your daughters? Whomever you have in the city, bring them out of this place, for we will spoil and destroy [Sodom]; for the outcry and shriek against its people has grown great before the Lord, and He has sent us to destroy it.
(Genesis 19:10–13)

Once I was deeply concerned about my son's whereabouts in the late night hours and began to pray for him, my face in the rug, weeping and crying out to our heavenly Father. What a good position to be in, for God shortly heard my cry and spoke: "Send his angel to get him!"

Therefore, I pointed in the direction I where I felt he was and said, "Please, go and get my son!" I began to praise God in relief for answered prayer and waited.

Shortly, in came the errant teenager as the birds were singing in the breaking dawn. I thanked *God* again for His help. Pausing, I glanced to my left, and standing there in a long, light gossamer gown that was gently blowing around his bare feet, was a huge angel, well over eight feet tall and three feet wide, going right up through the ceiling. We both stood motionless as I marveled at this miracle of compassion on a worried mother. My words to him were, "Thank you for getting my son," for I didn't know what else to say! Very soon, he quietly left and I could rest in peace, knowing I had the help I needed when in trouble.

Do you not know also that we [Christians] are to judge the [very] angels and pronounce opinion between right and wrong [for them]?
(1 Corinthians 6:3)

It is so important for us to cleanse our house with the precious blood of Jesus, shed for us and our protection, and then the place is considered sacred ground, and God will be free to come and go. All books that are questionable of horoscopes, witchcraft, Harry Potter, or any new age authors need to be removed. Then the house can be anointed with oil, free of Buddhas or any other idols that might be around. For with uncleanness come spirits of infirmities and sickness. Barrenness can also be a result of compromise. Masks from abroad, little imported dolls should all be examined in the light of the Holy Spirit, that trouble stays far away. "Have no idols before Me!" says the Lord.

When we are sure that everything in the house is pleasing to the Lord, we can apply the spiritual blood of the Lord Jesus to all the portals and believe that God will reveal what you need to do.

I once saw a wicked black spirit, eight feet tall, standing behind a neighbor who had trouble with epilepsy. With some counseling on his authority in God and his ability to command that spirit to leave him alone, the next time he came to the door, the wicked spirit was gone. Daily communion and anointing with oil are so important, for our blessing from God and our protection as well.

So be encouraged, dear ones, that we are always surrounded by our angels, ready to help us, no matter what the circumstance.

The Lord, the God of heaven, Who took me from my father's house, from the land of my family and my birth, Who spoke to me and swore to me, saying, To your offspring I will give this land—He will send His Angel before you, and you will take a wife from there for my son.
(Genesis 24:7)

There are always those dark days, when we have gone ahead of GOD, unwilling to wait on His perfect timing, and when we do that, we so often open ourselves up to the plots of the enemy of our soul, Hasaten, as my Jewish believing friends would say.

When working in a soup kitchen, showing myself useful, I forgot to check and see that the car insurance was updated. Coming back from a clothing pickup, I ran into the back of a car on the other side of a hill that was stalled in the middle of the street. This resulted in a financial crunch whereby I was required to repay in monthly increments. As I was walking toward the building where this was to be settled, I suddenly saw two angels, about my size in white gowns to their knees and barefoot, holding up my arms on either side. I believe that they were "Goodness" and "Mercy" by name, as it says in Psalm 23.

[Elisha] answered, Fear not; for those with us are more than those with them. Then Elisha prayed, Lord, I pray You, open his eyes that he may see. And the Lord opened the young man's eyes, and he saw, and behold, the mountain was full of horses and chariots of fire round about Elisha. And when the Syrians came down to him, Elisha prayed to the Lord, Smite this people with blindness, I pray You. And God smote them with blindness, as Elisha asked.
(2 Kings 6:16–18)

They shall bear you up on their hands, lest you dash your foot against a stone.
(Psalm 91:12)

Since Jesus delivered me from a cigarette habit many years ago, I have been an early morning runner. One day, just before going to a local church for daily prayer, I happened to glance behind me as I rounded a corner a block away. There I saw a long row of angels identically dressed in mid-length white gowns, in perfect formation, moving about a foot off the ground behind me. I felt remarkably assured as I progressed on my run in this bad neighborhood. However, when I rounded the corner farther down the street, there was a large, skinny, knobby, black, shadowy being in the middle of the street, legs crossed at the knees and hands on hips. I shrugged it off and jogged past him, only to suddenly hear the loud barking of a huge dog, who bared his teeth in a very menacing way at me. Fearful, but aware of what God had shown me earlier, I turned and said, "In the *Name of Jesus,* STOP!" The dog literally screeched to a halt, growling but immobile. I commanded him again to turn and go home, which he did, *in the Name of Jesus!*

What a relief to have been forewarned that morning that "there are many more with us than against us."

But when we cried to the Lord, He heard us and sent an angel.
(Numbers 20:16)

Of great concern to many during the Gulf War was the vulnerability of our troops in the Persian Gulf—no trees, just a lot of sand, and the possibility of nuclear war. Intercessors gathered, and we began to pray regularly every morning that God would spare our nation and the boys in this situation, as many of them were unsaved. As a result, they all received a New Testament, and God began to change the course of that mission. In particular, I remember my face in the rug, crying out to God, and suddenly I was in the Spirit high above the earth, looking down on Israel, which was being protected by two of the largest angels I have ever seen. They were circling Israel in an elliptical fashion, with their huge wings tucked at their sides, head to toe, so nothing could penetrate the atmosphere. Circling majestically at a very high speed, it was evident that nothing would pass them to do harm to the citizens who were at that very moment sitting in basements and cellars with gas masks on far below.

Scripture speaks of the angel Michael, "one of the chief

princes of Israel," in Daniel 10:13. And most certainly the other angel was Gabriel. Holy Scripture also says in Deuteronomy 32:8, "When God divided up the world among the nations, He gave each of them a supervising angel." These two angels were well over two hundred feet tall, and from my vantage point above them, I was fascinated by their power and grace. Our vision is so limited, *but God's vision is unlimited!*

*Surely goodness and
mercy will follow me all
the days of my life.*
(Psalm 23:6)

How often do we go beyond our physical bounds and wonder if God is going to be there to help us? Well, I had a chance to prove Him faithful one night on my way to work as a nurse on the night shift. I had very little sleep that day and was barely prepared for a night's work. As I got into my car, I said, "I'm too tired!" And with that, the whole car lit up with glory. I looked outside to see the whole car surrounded by cherubic Reubens-like angels, with curly hair (and very little clothing!). In this case, I needed ministering spirits to help me through—and He was faithful to me!

The chariots of God are twenty thousand, even thousands upon thousands. The Lord is among them as He was in Sinai, [so also] in the Holy Place (the sanctuary in Jerusalem).
(Psalm 68:17)

Possibly the more frequently seen angels are those who worship with us—how they love to praise God and are doing it around the throne on a daily, hourly, minute-by-minute basis! One early spring day, I turned off the phone, hung a "Do Not Disturb" sign on the door, and put on some music. I just began to sing to the Lord, the way we will someday be doing in heaven. The atmosphere began to change and the angels came, clustered all over the living room in long white gowns, some with hands upraised. It was hard to come back to reality and to see them go! Their song is higher, purer than human sound. When in corporate worship with no instruments and just the chorus "Hallelujah" of worship over and over, they will drown us out with their praise!

He let loose upon them the fierceness of His anger, His wrath and indignation and distress, by sending [a mission of] angels of calamity and woe among them.
(Psalm 78:49)

Once, when interceding for a dear sick relative, I began to hear the angels who were going to be taking her home. I knew, despite our prayers, that God wanted her to go to that heavenly celestial city to pray and encourage her husband and children from that side of the veil.

Again, ministering to a dear believer who was about the leave the earth, I saw the swirling white figures of angels in the bedroom, ready to take him to that place where there is no more sorrow or sighing, only joy.

Behold, I send an Angel before you to keep and guard you on the way and to bring you to the place I have prepared.
(Exodus 23:20)

When we are called to another task by the Spirit of God, He may send an angel to tell us something about the mission. I was on my way to Brazil when I was awakened one night by an angel, seven feet tall, standing immobile beside my bed. He impressed me with the thought that I was to encourage the young believers of that nation to do the work of the ministry and fulfill the call of God on their lives. Then he was gone.

*Bless (affectionately, gratefully praise) the Lord,
you His angels, you mighty ones who
do His commandments, hearkening
to the voice of His word.*
(Psalm 103:20)

When at the Washington for Jesus rally some years ago, the Lord spoke to me and said, "How can I bless this nation when the blood of the babies cries to Me from the ground?"

This was so disturbing to me that I felt committed to help as I could and began to get involved in counseling in front of an abortuary. But one very cold winter day, I was by myself as my partner had left, and I said to the Lord, "I hate to be out here alone!" And the Lord opened my eyes to see that I was not alone, for all around me in a tight circle were twenty-foot angels, with swords drawn and pointing upward to heaven. They were so tightly placed, shoulder to shoulder, that nothing could get between them and me, so I had the protection I needed in that sad place.

And they spoke of the God of Jerusalem as they spoke of the gods of the peoples of the earth, which are the work of the hands of men. For this cause Hezekiah the king and the prophet Isaiah son of Amoz prayed and cried to heaven. And the Lord sent an angel, who cut off all the mighty warriors and commanders and officers in the camp of the king of Assyria. So the Assyrian king returned with shamed face to his own land. And when he came into the house of his god, they who were his own offspring slew him there with the sword.
(2 Chronicles 32:19–21)

There was a day when I got off an airplane, with just enough time to catch another one to the next city, when the voice of my Father came: "You will be here for a while." I was very disappointed, and I went over to the huge plate-glass window, overlooking the runway, and began to pray hard in the Spirit. To my amazement, I looked outside and saw a long row of white-clad angels in perfect alignment, slowly lifting a thick white curtain of fog! As I prayed harder, the curtain went higher. However, because of my lack of tenacity in this situation, we were still delayed some time, but perhaps not as long as we would have been. It pays to pray with fervor until victory comes!

And in that vicinity there were shepherds living [out under the open sky] in the field, watching [in shifts] over their flock by night. And behold, an angel of the Lord stood by them, and the glory of the Lord flashed and shone all about them, and they were terribly frightened. But the angel said to them, Do not be afraid; for behold, I bring you good news of a great joy which will come to all the people. For to you is born this day in the town of David a Savior, Who is Christ (the Messiah) the Lord! And this will be a sign for you [by which you will recognize Him]: you will find [after searching] a Baby wrapped in swaddling clothes and lying in a manger. Then suddenly there appeared with the angel an army of the troops of heaven (a heavenly knighthood), praising God and saying, Glory to God in the highest [heaven], and on

*earth peace among men with whom He is well
pleased [men of goodwill, of His favor]. When
the angels went away from them into heaven,
the shepherds said one to another, Let us go
over to Bethlehem and see this thing (saying)
that has come to pass, which the Lord
has made known to us.*
(Luke 2:8–15)

In Florida, the citizens are prone to high tides that can cause a great deal of damage, and our little "dollhouse" was not exempt! One day, during hurricane season, the weatherman started to talk of a "storm surge." I noticed on my early morning walk that many people were packed to go to higher ground. When I got back to the house and went to the kitchen, I suddenly heard a strange rustling, as of paper. I turned to see four angels, about ten feet tall in long gowns, who were just folding their wings to their sides. Sensing they were awaiting instruction, I pointed toward the upcoming tide and said, "Angels, in the **Name of Jesus,** go and hold back that surge, so that no lives are lost and there will be no property damage!" I shared this with people at our fellowship that day, and we continued to pray the rest of Sunday afternoon. No damage or loss of life occurred. ***Wonderful Jesus!***

*For He will give His angels [espe-
cial] charge over you to accompany and defend and preserve you
in all your ways [of obedience
and service].*
(Psalm 91:11)

Dear little two-year-old Gladys, with her sweet little arms made for hugging, didn't really deserve the less-than-perfect circumstances she was in. Her father had contracted AIDS, and little Gladys was born with this dreadful disease. Because the whole family needed help, I was there for a short and poignant time. Her "Poppy" died, and soon thereafter it was Gladys's turn to meet her Creator. One lovely Christmas Eve, with lights on the tree and strung all around the ceiling, and on the TV a lovely Christmas special, fitting for the birth of the Messiah, the angel who was to escort Gladys to her "Poppy" and her Abba Father came and stood next to me. I was awed by his majestic size, for he was well over ten feet tall and two feet wide. In his full-length gown and majestic silence, I couldn't help thinking of those who came from heaven to announce the birth of Jesus, our Messiah, long ago in Bethlehem and that perhaps this angel had also witnessed that great event. Gladys was going to that place where there is no more sorrow or crying, but only joy.

Then war broke out in heaven; Michael and his angels went forth to battle with the dragon, and the dragon and his angels fought.
(Revelation 12:7)

After this I looked and a vast host appeared which no one could count, [gathered out] of every nation, from all tribes and peoples and languages. These stood before the throne and before the Lamb; they were attired in white robes, with palm branches in their hands. In loud voice they cried, saying, [Our] salvation is due to our God, Who is seated on the throne, and to the Lamb [to Them we owe our deliverance]! And all the angels were standing round the throne and round the elders [of the heavenly Sanhedrin] and the four living creatures, and they fell prostrate before the throne and worshiped God.
(Revelation 7:9–11)

Have you made the decision to follow Jesus yet? May I suggest to you that right now is a good time. It will be as though a great weight has rolled off your back. He has come to "heal the brokenhearted and set the captives free." There is no greater Friend than Jesus, so why not say this:

> "Dear Jesus, Thank You for going to the Cross of Calvary for me and taking all my sins and sickness on Your Body that day. Come into my heart and forgive me. And thank You for this new life. Amen."

> Welcome to the wonderful family of God!

*But during the night an angel of the Lord
opened the prison doors and, leading them out,
said, Go, take your stand in the temple courts
and declare to the people the whole doctrine
concerning this Life (the eternal life
which Christ revealed).*
(Acts 5:19–20)

For your protection, pray this psalm:

He who dwells in the secret place of the Most High shall remain stable and fixed under the shadow of the Almighty [Whose power no foe can withstand].

I will say of the Lord, He is my Refuge and my Fortress, my God; on Him I lean and rely, and in Him I [confidently] trust!

For [then] He will deliver you from the snare of the fowler and from the deadly pestilence.

[Then] He will cover you with His pinions, and under His wings shall you trust and find refuge; His truth and His faithfulness are a shield and a buckler.

You shall not be afraid of the terror of the night, nor of the arrow (the evil plots and slanders of the wicked) that flies by day,

Nor of the pestilence that stalks in darkness, nor of the destruction and sudden death that surprise and lay waste at noonday.

A thousand may fall at your side, and ten thousand at your right hand, but it shall not come near you.

Only a spectator shall you be [yourself inaccessible in the secret place of the Most High] as you witness the reward of the wicked.

Because you have made the Lord your refuge, and the Most High your dwelling place,

There shall no evil befall you, nor any plague or calamity come near your tent.

For He will give His angels [especial] charge over you to accompany and defend and preserve you in all your ways [of obedience and service].

They shall bear you up on their hands, lest you dash your foot against a stone.

You shall tread upon the lion and adder; the young lion and the serpent shall you trample underfoot.

Because he has set his love upon Me, therefore will I deliver him; I will set him on high, because he knows and understands My name [has a personal knowledge of My mercy, love, and kindness—trusts and relies on Me, knowing I will never forsake him, no, never].

He shall call upon Me, and I will answer him; I will be with him in trouble, I will deliver him and honor him.

With long life will I satisfy him and show him My salvation. (Psalm 91)

Printed in the USA
CPSIA information can be obtained
at www.ICGtesting.com
LVHW052348220823
756022LV00004BA/103